ECCLESIASTES

SEARCHING FOR THE SILVER LININGS

Dan Blazer

STREAMS of MERCY
study series

Ecclesiastes: *Searching for the Silver Linings*

HillCrest
PUBLISHING

1648 Campus Ct.
Abilene, TX 79601
www.hillcrestpublishing.com

Cover Design and Layout by Sarah Bales Design

Printed in the United States of America

ISBN 0-89112-255-9

1,2,3,4,5

TABLE OF CONTENTS

DEDICATION

To Gordon and Lora Lee's Tuesday Evening Home Study Group

Campbell Church of Christ

Campbell, California

Thank you so much for your warm fellowship, love, and service
during our year worshipping with you.

FOR TEACHERS AND CLASS LEADERS...

The word of God is powerful. This belief is the driving force behind the Streams of Mercy Study Series. Assigned reading, brief commentary, and questions for reflection and class discussion are presented for each section of the biblical book. The goal is changed lives–changed by the power of the Word.

Consider the following suggestions as you prepare for class:

- Even though class members may have read the passage assigned for the week, select some verses to be read aloud in class: let the Word speak.

- Give a brief summary of the points made in the lesson, then begin working with the questions. As you prepare for your class, explore the possibility of a variety of answers to the questions. Don't be afraid of momentary silence when you ask the questions; give people a chance to think, but be prepared to prompt the discussion.

- Be creative with your classroom time. Sometimes have the class work in small groups to discuss the questions. Consider having someone prepare to comment on a particular question for the next scheduled class meeting. Perhaps you could ask someone to be prepared to share his or her experience with finding time to work on the lesson in the middle of work and family obligations—in this way we acknowledge the struggle to make time for Bible study. Give someone the task of praying for the whole class throughout the coming week as they all find time for study. Let the class know this will be happening.

- Ask class members to make a plan of action that puts into practice the things the text calls for. This may be a service project or a commitment to pray for help in overcoming specific problems the text brings to light. Be prepared to suggest plans of action and to get the class involved in brainstorming about this. Avoid taking charge too much; let the class get involved.

- Find out if anyone in the class would like to create banners or any kind of visuals pertaining to the study. This is a good way to validate the gifts of others.

- Try to inspire excitement about the class working together each week to hear and understand the word of God. Stress that this is one of the ways we are in fellowship with one another.

- Be sensitive to people who don't want to speak in class. Encourage those who want to speak, but who may be a little tentative. Practice good leadership by not allowing any one person to dominate the discussions.

- Try to keep the discussions on target. One complaint we often hear about Bible classes is that the group too easily gets off the subject. These volumes are designed to promote discussion of the biblical text. Pray for help to keep the class focused without preventing healthy discussion.

Nothing is more important than seeking God's guidance as you prepare for class. Ask him to open your heart so the text speaks to you and convicts you, then you will be more prepared to lead the group. May the Lord bless all of you as you seek his will, and may you know the everflowing streams of his mercy.

> Of making many books there is no end, and much study wearies the body.
> Ecclesiastes 12:12

The Editors

INTRODUCTION

Want a good devotional book to cheer you up? Need encouragement during a time of difficulty? Searching for some good advice? Read *How to Win Friends and Influence People* or *The Power of Positive Thinking*. This Old Testament book may have stood the test of time, but it is difficult at first glance to understand why *anyone* would choose to read Ecclesiastes rather than read the psalms of David or the beatitudes of Christ. The book seems more at home among the melancholy meditations of the stoic Greek philosophers than among the sacred writings of both Jews and Christians. So why should any good Christian pay attention to Ecclesiastes?

Ecclesiastes, on the surface, sheds little light upon our complex and threatening world. In fact, the writer appears to cloud what light we have. He sees only "clouds [that] return after the rain" (12:2). Ecclesiastes exposes the evil in each of us: "All labor and all achievement spring from man's envy of his neighbor" (4:4). The writer exposes the inadequacy of our knowledge: "For with much wisdom comes much sorrow" (1:18). We attempt to calm our anxieties; the writer exposes them. We find answers to our questions; the writer questions our answers. We reflect that life is good; the writer declares "reflect again." We look for hope; the writer cries "meaningless." We search for a good guidebook; the writer pronounces, "Of making many books there is no end, and much study wearies the body" (12:12).

In other words, the writer of Ecclesiastes thwarts us at every turn in our pursuit of happiness and hope. He "rains on our parade" and then clouds our attempts to escape the rain. Why should we pay attention to this gray and depressing book? Because the writer exposes silver linings within those same clouds. Not every cloud has a silver lining, as the old saying goes, but we find many silver linings in Ecclesiastes. We benefit from Ecclesiastes by discovering these silver linings. The writer informs us, ever so subtly, that we find meaning in the apparent meaninglessness of life. That meaning is the all-powerful God, creator and sustainer of the universe.

Who was the author of Ecclesiastes? A quick read of the first few verses strongly suggests that King Solomon, son of David, was the author and, for the purposes of this short study, let's go with that. Solomon was given all he could hope to possess. He asked for wisdom, and he received both wisdom and riches (1 Kings 3:4-15).

> Why should we pay attention to the gray and depressing book of Ecclesiastes? Because the writer exposes silver linings within the dark clouds.

Possessing wisdom and wealth, inheriting a powerful kingdom at peace with its neighbors, surely Solomon would be the greatest of all kings of Israel! The title of the book designates the author, but not by name. In Hebrew (Ecclesiastes in the Greek), he is the Qoheleth, the preacher; that is, Solomon is the teacher who convenes the congregation. When he calls the people together near the end of his life, what does he have to say?

Solomon was anything but encouraging in his summation about life: "Everything is meaningless" (1:2). Hope has disappeared: "All his days his work is pain and grief" (2: 25). The congregation could not be assured of their future: "As fish are caught in a cruel net...so men are trapped by evil times that fall unexpectedly upon them" (9:12). And in the end, "the dust returns to the ground it came from" (12:7).

> The attempts by the Preacher to do good were foiled: "When I surveyed all that my hands had done... everything was meaningless, a chasing after the wind" (Ecclesiastes 2:11).

Yet even as he paints this depressing picture, Solomon recognizes a truth which many of us forget: "Fear God and keep his commandments, for this is the whole duty of man" (12:13). All too often, we look to God for immediate gratification. We view God as a "sugar daddy," a year-round Santa Claus. We falsely equate grace with gratification, joy with giddiness, peace with prosperity. Solomon warns us that we must think again about our view of God

> Ecclesiastes is grouped in the Old Testament among the "books of wisdom"; yet, it is a strange book of wisdom indeed! "For the wise man, like the fool, will not be long remembered" (2:16). Two kinds of wisdom can be found in the Old Testament: **speculative wisdom** (answering basic questions about life) and **proverbial wisdom** (short sayings and rules for personal happiness and well-being). Solomon interspersed speculative wisdom and proverbial wisdom throughout Ecclesiastes.
> ▯

and our relationship with God. If we accept the will of the Lord, if we accept his grace, then we must also accept his transcendence: "God is in heaven and you are on earth" (5:2). Only then will we find the silver lining among the clouds that darken our lives.

How can we discover the silver linings in Ecclesiastes? We must, fellow student, read carefully. At times we must read between the lines, search for the silver linings within the clouds Solomon paints. Join me now as we search the words of the wisest King of all. Come, let us listen to the Preacher.

1
WHY EVEN BOTHER?
Ecclesiastes 1:1-2:26

Everything is Meaningless

God gave Solomon both wisdom and wealth (1 Kings 3:10-13). Which of the two was more likely to create problems for him? Wealth, you say. After all, "the love of money is a root of all kinds of evil" (1 Timothy 6:10). No. Worldly wisdom brought this king as much grief as worldly wealth. Solomon was a man of the world, a man who possessed the talents and opportunities to make a difference. He not only reflected upon life; he attacked life through the pursuit of its pleasures and projects. Solomon possessed it all, experienced it all, did it all. What were the fruits of perhaps the most "full" life ever lived?

If Ecclesiastes is an accurate window into

The life of Solomon is somewhat like Goethe's fictitious life of Faust. Faust made a bargain with the Devil, but not the bargain most people imagine. He didn't sell his soul for pleasure. Faust bargained, "Give me every pleasure imaginable. If I, at any time, find myself bored, empty, and desiring no more pleasures, then my soul is yours to do with as you choose." Goethe's Faust, like Solomon (Ecclesiastes 12:1-8) eventually tired of the world's pleasure.

Solomon's life, he lived his final years profoundly dejected, depressed, and depleted. Nothing mattered at the conclusion of the matter.

Solomon warned his readers about the way to live life, even as he concluded that everything was meaningless. Don't seek fulfillment in past accomplishments. Don't search for hope in the future of this world. Don't expect your work to pay off in your favor. Rather, seek wisdom. Through wisdom, God grants happiness. What God grants is sufficient (1:24).

> Solomon reminded his subjects of their days wandering in the wilderness. During those days, the people were granted a day's supply of manna and quail: "I will rain down bread from heaven for you. The people were to go out each day and gather enough for that day" (Exodus 16:4). One day's supply was enough.

Ecclesiastes 1:1-18
All Things are Wearisome

Years ago, I saw a movie, *Charly*, that portrayed a man who was mentally retarded, yet quite happy. He behaved like a child, and he enjoyed life as does a carefree child. Through the magic of science, this man was given a potion that transformed him into a genius. With his newfound knowledge and wisdom, he surveyed the world and found it wanting, sadly wanting. He became cynical and depressed. The potion eventually lost its effect, returning him to his original retarded state, a state in which he once again found happiness. Solomon also appears to have known too much, to have understood at such a deep level that he became cynical. He saw the world as it truly was—and he found everything meaningless. We work, but we don't see the value of labor. Worldly wisdom leads to a gloomy picture of life, according to Solomon.

Can we find a silver lining in this gloomy picture? Should we purposefully dull our minds so that we might remain blissful like Charly? *Is ignorance bliss?* If we're drawn to reflection, if God views the big picture through the eyes of worldly wisdom, then the state of the world might indeed appear bleak. Yet we must view the world through the eyes that God has provided, eyes that assure us that he is in charge. As Solomon's father David saw, "The heavens declare the glory of God; the skies proclaim the work of his hands" (Psalms 19:1). The silver lining is to be found by taking a God's-eye view.

> Solomon, though he couldn't always quite grasp the presence of God, recognized his own folly in seeking worldly wisdom: "For with much wisdom comes much sorrow; the more knowledge, the more grief."
> Ecclesiastes 1:18

▯ Reflection and Application

1. Have you ever experienced a time when you knew more than you wanted to? Share this with the group.

2. Should we seek after wisdom? If so, how do we avoid the problem Solomon experienced?

NEXT

Ecclesiastes 2:1-11
He Undertook Great Projects

A few years ago, my wife and I walked across the Brooklyn Bridge. Though it was completed well over a century ago and is far from the largest suspension bridge in the world today, it remains an impressive feat of design and construction. Who built the bridge? The chief architect engineer was a man named Roebling, yet few remember him.

Few of us will build anything as remarkable as the Brooklyn Bridge. None of us will complete projects that could come close to competing with the projects of King Solomon. Yet when all was said and done, even Solomon concluded that his efforts were a "chasing after the wind; nothing was gained under the sun" (2:11).

Can we find joy in building? Yes. Solomon reveals the silver lining to this cloud. First, he was commissioned to build the temple of the Lord, not Solomon's temple (1 Kings 6:1). Of more importance, Solomon reminds us in Psalm 127:1, "Unless the Lord builds the house, its builders labor in vain." If the temple was Solomon's temple, then Solomon could find no pleasure, no sense of accomplishment in completing the task. On the other hand, if he allowed himself to become the hands of the Lord, then the completion of that building was not in vain.

☐ Reflection and Application

1. Recall something that you accomplished years ago and in which you took great pride. How meaningful is that accomplishment today?

2. In what ways are you not your own?

Ecclesiastes 2:12-2:16
The Wise Man Will Not Long Be Remembered

We can gather so much knowledge about something that we end up missing the big picture. During ancient times, the astronomer Ptolemy worked out an elaborate system to follow the progress of the heavenly bodies. The system predicted almost perfectly the paths of the planets and stars. Many stood in amazement at the intricacies of such "wisdom." Ptolemy even recognized that the earth was not flat but rather was a sphere. Only years later did Copernicus discover a slight problem with Ptolemy's system. Ptolemy put the earth at the center of the universe! He couldn't see the truth of the movement of the heavenly bodies because he was so deeply involved in the details of his system. Today most of us remember Copernicus (and later Galileo), but most of us do not remember Ptolemy.

Worldly wisdom is like that. For a time, we *appear* to be more knowledgeable than those around us. But eventually "the same fate overtakes them both" (2:14), both the knowledgeable and the ordinary. Although this is not a comforting thought, Solomon, discovers a silver lining to this cloud. Over time, only *heavenly wisdom* will be remembered. We will always remember the wisdom God granted King David, who said, "The Lord is my shepherd, I shall lack nothing" (Psalm 23:1).

Reflection and Application

1. Try to recall from your past some advice that you received, advice that seemed wise at the time, but later proved harmful.

2. Consider some of the advice you give your children, friends, and family. Have you always been as wise as you thought you were at the time?

Ecclesiastes 2:17-2:26
All His Days His Work is Pain

Most of us will spend a good portion of our adult lives at work, either in the home or in the workplace. We work hard, and we expect results. We expect rewards. Solomon didn't paint a pretty picture of work. He hated life because of work (2:17); yet it is through work that humankind is to find pleasure (3:13). Solomon presents a paradox to the reader. As much as we at times dread our work, the only way we can be happy with our work is to enjoy it. If we work to please God, he, in turn, blesses us with happiness in our work (2:26).

☐ Reflection and Application

1. Do you find yourself at times both resentful of the work you do, yet thankful that you have a job? How can we reconcile such conflicting feelings?

2. What is your response to Solomon when he says "A man can do nothing better than to eat and drink and find satisfaction in his work"?

A Closer Look

Solomon was a complex character. Perhaps we should expect nothing less from a man who was the wisest ever to live. He knew *about* God. But did he know God? We can know much about God, only to feel empty within, alienated from God and the world around us. Solomon is a character more to be pitied than to be envied. Doesn't this sound strange? Don't *we* pray for what Solomon possessed?

NEXT → Feb, 2, 2026

2
WHAT TIME IS IT?
Ecclesiastes 3:1-15

A Time for Everything

Solomon, nearing the end of his time on this earth, asks "What time is it?" He wasn't so much interested in the time of day as the time of *life*. His personal "season" (3:1) is late autumn, perhaps early winter. The key emotional task we must complete in late life is "integration," that is, sorting through the events of our lives and making sense of those events. We must review our lives so that the story of our lives makes sense.

Have you noticed how often older people reminisce? Perhaps they are working to tell their story, to make sense of the ebb and flow of their lives.

Solomon guided his readers through sorting the events of our lives. There is a season for every activity (3:1). There are times we should save something

> There is a tide in the affairs of men,
> Which taken at the flood, leads on to fortune;
> Omitted, all the voyage of their life
> Is bound in shallows and in miseries.
> -Shakespeare, *Julius Caesar* 4.3

[]

instead of throwing it away, such as an old photograph (3:6). On the other hand, we often should give away things we have saved, such as clothes hanging in our closets that we have not worn for years. Over time, things should balance out.

So what are we to make of the seasons of life? Are we simply to accept the good and the bad, the ups and downs, and muddle through? Must we be resigned to fate? Do we have only a few opportunities in life? Can we find hope amid this dreariness?

Solomon informs us that there is a silver lining. In spite of the ups and downs, the give and take, even the contradictions of our lives, God has given us a higher view. There may be a time for every opportunity, but we must step out of time. He doesn't wish us simply to go with the flow, he wishes us to grasp eternity! Time is not an easy concept to fathom. God, however, encourages us to step into a fourth dimension with him—*eternity*. Eternity is not immortality, an indefinite extension of time into the future. Eternity, the fourth dimension, is *outside time*, a time when time shall

> We think of time as having three dimensions, like a videocassette tape that projects events as it plays itself out. There is a *past* (the tape that has already been played), a *present* (the tape being played), and a *future* (the tape that will be played). God, however, encourages us to step into a fourth dimension—*eternity*, a dimension outside time, when time shall be no more.
>
> ▯

be no more. Eternity is God's time. It puts the other dimensions of time in perspective—God's perspective.

Ecclesiastes 3:1-8
There is a Season for Every Activity

Most of us believe that we need more time. We can't find enough hours in the day to complete all the tasks we set for ourselves. We look at our watches 100 times a day. We try to control time, yet time seems to control us. Solomon reminded us that time cannot be controlled. Even as we look to eternity, we must go with the flow of time. Of course, we must plan and watch our watches. How can we do otherwise and survive in this world? Yet things happen for which we cannot plan, happenings both good and bad. We are invited to a party that we don't expect to enjoy. Suddenly we realize we're having great fun. We laugh when we expect to weep (3:4) and speak up at times when we expect to keep quiet (3:7). Time is a gift—and we cannot control a gift.

For every one of us, there is a time—for everything.

□ Reflection and Application

1. Think about "a time to tear down and a time to build up" (3:3). Can you remember a time in your life when you kept trying to make something work,

even though it was evident to others that it just wasn't going to work? Did you finally give up? How did you finally decide?

2. Have you ever attempted to write an account of your life, perhaps a journal or reflection? In what ways does your life make sense when you think back and in what ways does it not make sense?

Ecclesiastes 3:9-11
He has set eternity in the hearts of men

Solomon addressed the age-old philosophical question, "What is beauty?" Beauty is found in the creation, a timeless beauty. Yet even that beauty must be seen in perspective. We must step back to witness God's beauty, back to the perspective of eternity. We drive along a beautiful road, looking at a mountain rising out of the ocean and reaching to the sky. We see God outside time having created this timeless wonder. Or we're troubled because of financial problems and need to speak to a wise friend. That friend says something that brings immediate comfort and security. Where is the source of that comfort? Somewhere outside time, for wisdom seems timeless.

Even so, his majesty extends to the future beyond

> At times, God permits us to see the world through the eyes of eternity.

our view. He reveals himself; yet he remains a mystery to us—even as he lifts us above our mundane experiences. The silver lining to the cloudy mystery of the ways of God is found in his revelation *and* his mystery. A god who can be embraced is not a god who can save us. Such a god would be too small.

⬚ Reflection and Application

1. Try to imagine a time when you were dramatically struck by something that was beautiful. How does this experience of beauty seem "timeless"?

2. How would you define eternity? How does thinking about eternity make you feel?

Ecclesiastes 3:12-15
There is Nothing Better for Men Than to Be Happy and to Do Good

How are we to respond to this mystery of eternity that we can half-glimpse and find half-hidden from us? We must take pleasure in the time God has given us in the present: "This is the day the Lord has made; let us rejoice and be glad in it" (Psalm 118:24). Daily pleasure comes from enjoying the simple things of life, such as eating, drinking, and working. How often do we hurry through a meal, gulping down our food because we are rushing to another activity? How often do we watch the clock at work, so we can race home to a meal (which we then gulp down so we can...)? We frequently take no pleasure in the moment because we are constantly hastening to the next moment. We don't "stop and smell the flowers." We try to crowd so much into our lives that we cannot enjoy what is so readily available to us. Is there something more to life than a harried, dark rush through life? Yes.

God has set eternity into our hearts by revealing Christ to our sinful hearts. As Solomon wrote, "nothing can be added to it and nothing taken from it" (3:14).

☐ Reflection and Application

How much can we trust Solomon's advice for finding happiness, given that Solomon was not a happy man?

A Closer Look

Solomon knew that we would never find peace on this earth, that we would never find continual happiness. Eternity does not exist in temporal time. Perhaps no ruler in history possessed a greater opportunity to alter history, to tip the balance to security and peace. This great king, however, realized that, at the end, even he couldn't bring peace. He was correct. Following his death, the Israelite kingdom split into warring factions, the northern and southern kingdoms. Peace doesn't forever replace war in three-dimensional time. Peace comes only in eternity.

Next Feb 3

3
WILL I EVER FIND JUSTICE?
Ecclesiastes 3:16–4:3

In the Place of Judgment – Wickedness

Solomon complains that God doesn't care if humans witness evil prevailing over good. The wise king, over his lifetime, witnessed what he believed to be great injustices, injustices that should have brought retribution.

Solomon's complaint, if we think about it, is ironic. God granted him a life of peace and prosperity. He lived an extravagant lifestyle, one that couldn't be supported by the income from his subjects. His extravagance led to social discontent and disruption of his kingdom (1 Kings 10:14-29, 12:4-19). His wives turned his heart away from God and, in his old age, he built idols to other gods (1 Kings 11:4, 5). Even so, God didn't bring total defeat to Solomon: "I will not take the whole kingdom out of Solomon's hand; I have made him ruler all the days of his life for the sake of David my servant" (1 Kings 11:54). Who was Solomon to speak of injustice? He received far more good during his life than he deserved. Can we learn anything from the writings of a king who implies that God treats us like animals? (3:18)

Ecclesiastes 3:16-22
God Brings Justice to All

Somehow, even during his despair, Solomon found a silver lining of sorts. He realized, as Job was forced to realize, that the ways of God are above the ways of men. Solomon came to understand that we simply cannot know the ways of the Lord (3:16). God alone is the author of justice, and somehow God will judge both the righteous and the wicked. Nevertheless, Solomon had no hope that he would witness that judgment nor appreciate the grace of God during his lifetime. Rather, he saw no farther than the vicious "law of the wild" – man's fate is like that of the animals (3:19).

When we witness a tragedy, perhaps an ongoing tragedy such as drought, famine, and tribal warfare in parts of northern Africa, we seek answers. We want to understand. In order to make sense out of the senseless, we make our own judgments. Perhaps we see things balancing out: "Africa has experienced periods of drought and famine before. Things will get better in the future." Perhaps we view God's judgment in our terms: "The political situation surely is a major contributor to Africa's problems. If the despotic rulers in some African countries could be removed, then their problems would be solved."

I think we judge the events around us in order to make sense of them. The silver lining that Solomon leaves for us is that, despite our most conscientious efforts to make sense out of the senseless, we will never make sense of the events around us. If we are honest, it does seem at times that the "law of the wild" predominates. Good people in the world *don't* seem to have an advantage. God's ways are above our own.

☐ Reflection and Application

1. We live in an intensely competitive work environment. "Survival of the fittest" seems to be the norm. How does this "system" coexist with our great God?

2. What do you think Solomon meant when he said, "man has no advantage over the animals" (3:19)? Does he imply that animals have a soul—or that we don't? Does he believe that we are basically instinctual creatures?

Ecclesiastes 4:1-3
I saw the tears of the oppressed

Most of us have imagined Solomon secure in his palace, enjoying the wealth around him. He doesn't appear to have been overly concerned about the welfare of others. We read in 1 Kings 9:15 that Solomon forced the labor of thousands to build not only the temple but also his palace. Who was Solomon to become depressed about the oppression of others?

Wisdom is a fickle gift. It can be a curse as well as a blessing. At times we see more than we want to. Solomon was too wise to overlook the inequities around him—even though he was responsible for many of those inequities. Yet his response wasn't guilt, but rather sympathy. Worldly wisdom is like that. It opens our eyes, but doesn't necessarily convict us. He didn't feel a sense of responsibility for the oppression of others. He didn't lift the burden from his subjects.

> The misery around Solomon led him at times to wish that he were dead, for "the dead...are happier than the living."
> Ecclesiastes 4:2

How do we find comfort when observing inequities and oppression around us? To find comfort, we must become active in comforting the oppressed. Unlike Solomon, we must accept our responsibilities. If we accept our responsibility, then we are motivated to do what we can to correct the problem.

I find it incongruous that this wise, wealthy, and most powerful ruler was so blind to ways in which he might have become a comforter. Solomon saw the problem but didn't see that he was part of the problem—and therefore he didn't see that he was part of the solution. We feel better when we are part of the solution, even if we are only a small part.

1. Most of us reflect at times on the world situation and become depressed about its almost overwhelming problems. Do you ever feel that you have contributed to those problems? If so, how?

2. Does benevolent work in your community at times appear of no value? Are you tempted to give up? Why do you, at times, continue your efforts even when giving to others seems to make no difference?

Ecclesiastes 4:4-12
Alone in a cut-throat world

To Solomon, the world was a cut-throat, competitive place. We don't "get ahead" in the world by cooperating with neighbors (4:1). We get ahead by envying our neighbors and trying to outdo them (4:4). Solomon, however, sees the foolishness of unbridled competition. Does having more make us feel better? Not necessarily. At times we feel more at peace when we're willing to do with less (4:6). If we devote all our energies to getting ahead, we find ourselves lonely (4:8a). Of course, we accumulate more if we put our own needs above those of others. But remember, "it's

21

lonely at the top" and a meaningless, miserable business (4:8b).

Solomon informed his readers that there is a silver lining to the grim world of the marketplace. That lining is relationships with others. Two are better than one (4:9). We may be more efficient if we work alone but if something goes wrong, we find ourselves without someone to help us (4:10). If we choose not to share our blanket with another, we find ourselves cold for we cannot share the warmth of others (4:11). If we stubbornly maintain our independence and refuse to cooperate with others, we become weak and vulnerable and make enemies. Three strings woven together are stronger than one alone (4:12). Solomon was a lonely man; after all, powerful kings don't have many confidants. Building the temple and palaces in Jerusalem didn't build the king a network of supportive and caring friends.

☐ Reflection and Application

1. Do you agree with Solomon that the way to get ahead in the world is to go it alone? Explain your answer.

2. How can we balance the conflict between making tough business decisions while maintaining our integrity and having good relations with others?

Ecclesiastes 4:13-16
Better to Be a Poor Youth

This passage is one of the more obscure in Ecclesiastes (and Ecclesiastes is not an easily understood book). What Solomon feared was that he would be forgotten. Wisdom and wealth can provide much, yet they cannot purchase immortality. They didn't assure Solomon that he would be loved in his latter years. In fact, just the opposite occurred. The older king found the young competing for his throne and gaining influence over the populace. To make matters worse, these young successors scuttled many of the accomplishments of King Solomon, further erasing and tarnishing his reputation. Solomon's son, Rehoboam, couldn't maintain the powerful kingdom his father had built. During his reign, the kingdom was divided. Solomon's grand enterprise was demolished within a generation.

▢ Reflection and Application

1. How do you believe the people felt about Solomon after his death?

2. Read 1 Kings, chapter 11. Do you believe Solomon was predicting the revolts against his kingdom or testifying that these revolts had already occurred? Explain your answer.

A Closer Look

Solomon, near the end of his life, looked around and saw injustice virtually everywhere. The fate of the righteous was no different than the fate of the wicked, there was no comfort for the oppressed, and entrepreneurs looking to their own needs neglected relationships with others. To add insult to injury, Solomon realized that the people would forget him and follow the younger generation, even though the younger generation was to scuttle the powerful and rich kingdom he built.

Solomon couldn't admit his own failure. He couldn't see how he might have contributed to the problems that he witnessed. Mistakes are difficult to admit, especially when those mistakes span decades of our lives. Yet how can we ever see the glory of God if we don't see the sinfulness of our own nature? Herein lies the silver lining. To feel good about our lives, we must be honest about them. It appears that Solomon never took responsibility to correct the injustices that he himself had created.

Next

Feb. 4

4
HOW MUCH MONEY
IS ENOUGH?
Ecclesiastes 5:1-6:12

The Power of God and the Power of Money

Solomon, despite his dejection (*all is meaningless*)
and resignation (*man is like the animals*), remained
in awe of the majesty of God. In fact, he found himself
at a loss for words when thinking about God. He
hastened to quiet others who might speak too freely
(5:2). If we read between the lines, however, we learn
that while Solomon may have been overwhelmed by the
power of God, he simply didn't have a close relationship
with God. His father, David, was in awe at the power of
God (Psalm 19:1). However, David speaks with God:
"To you, O Lord, I lift up my soul; in you I trust; O my
God. Do not let me be put to shame, nor let my enemies
triumph over me" (Psalm 25:2). Solomon recognized
the power of God, yet he felt stymied in calling upon
that power. Solomon trusted money for much of his
life. After all, money *appeared* to serve him well: he
had a close relationship with money; others stood in
awe of his money; the queen of Sheba, while visiting
Solomon, exclaimed, "Not even half was told me;
in wisdom and wealth you have far exceeded the

report I heard" (1 Kings 10:7). Wealth, however, didn't bring contentment (5:10). Luxury didn't help him sleep at night (5:12). Do we trust God or money? Do we feel closer to God or to our money? Will we, in the end, rebuke ourselves if we fail to develop a close relationship with God because we put our faith in money?

> Whoever loves money never has money enough.
> Ecclesiastes 5:10
> ☐

Ecclesiastes 5:1-7
Stand in Awe of God

The God we glimpse in Ecclesiastes 1–4 is far above, and we are earthbound. Solomon advises us that we must recognize and respect that distance. We must watch our steps and watch our speech. Solomon probably refers to an old proverb in 5:3. Foolish people go on and on with their ramblings, just as the troubled person ruminates about the day's worries over and over at night. In our ramblings, we make promises. But we don't need to be too quick to make such promises. Failing to keep the vows we make is worse than making the vow in the first place. Better to keep our distance, to stand in awe. Don't fool around with God!

> The abundance of a rich man permits him no sleep.
> Ecclesiastes 5:12
> ☐

We can, however, find a silver lining in Solomon's gloomy picture of God. The wise king reminds us not to become too familiar with God. God is not our "pappy."

He is not a "sugar daddy." He is not just a good buddy. No Old Testament character had a closer relationship with God than David, who writes in Psalm 8, "When I consider your heavens, the work of your fingers, the moon and the stars, which you have set in place, what is man that you are mindful of him?" Regardless of how close and comforting a relationship we develop with God, God remains God, and we remain his creatures.

☐ Reflection and Application

1. How might we become too "familiar" with God?

2. Some theologians have suggested that our concept of God as **immanent** (that he is everywhere around us) has triumphed over our concept of God as **transcendent** (that he is separate and apart from us). What do immanent and transcendent mean to you in relation to God? Do you agree with these theologians?

Ecclesiastes 5:8-20
We Never Have Enough Money

Solomon surely knew both the power and the problems of money. He knew the power of the marketplace. People who possess worldly wisdom know how to make money, how to save money, and how to help others make money. "A good man leaves an inheritance to his children's children, but the sinner's wealth is laid up for the righteous" (Proverbs 12:22). Even the king profits if others profit (5:9). What could possibly be wrong with wealth?

The wealthiest man of that time was not at all convinced that wealth was in fact an advantage. He sees a cloud over the sunny skies of prosperity. Solomon's silver lining comes in the form of a warning. Riches are meaningless. Why? People are out for themselves in a totally competitive, dog-eat-dog world. Those not so fortunate will be oppressed. Yet the problems don't end with the oppressed. Regardless of where you are in the hierarchy, someone is always higher than you and is watching you, ready to strip you of your wealth. Even the king takes advantage of those immediately under him (5:8, 9).

Paul wrote that "the love of money is a root of all kinds of evil" (1 Timothy 6:10), and wise king Solomon informed us *why* such love brings evil and misery. First, if we love money, we never seem to have enough (5: 10). Once we get those goods into our homes, we become dissatisfied with them (5:11). Finally, we come to realize that we can't take our possessions with us beyond the grave (5:15).

Better, wrote Solomon, to find satisfaction in a simple meal and something to quench our thirst after a hard day's work. Worldly wisdom begets wealth and serves wealth. If by chance we are blessed with possessions and we can enjoy them in peace, then that peace is surely a gift from God. On their own, however, these possessions can never bring us peace or joy (5:19).

The secret to enjoying our possessions is not to become focused upon them. We must focus on our work. If we focus on our work, possessions become a pleasant distraction, not an obsession (5:18, 20). If he were living today, I think Solomon might say something like "You can't really enjoy that easy chair unless you have spent the day in hard labor" and "You can't enjoy a good meal unless you have contributed food to the table of someone who is not as fortunate as you."

☐ Reflection and Application

1. If you are like most people, you might believe that you would be happier if you possessed something you currently don't. Think for a moment. What possessions would lead you to say, "This is enough. I don't need anything more"?

2. How often do you think about money? What are some of the different ways in which you think about money each day, such as paying bills?

Ecclesiastes 6:1-12
How long is long enough to live?

Solomon, in chapter 6 of Ecclesiastes, dips deeper into his despair (6:7-11). He describes people who cannot enjoy almost anything. The inability to enjoy, the inability to feel pleasure, is one of the most hopeless and disturbing feelings imaginable. When a person cannot feel, cannot find any pleasure in life, then life is not worth living. She doesn't care what happens to her. Suicidal thoughts may surface. The pain of not feeling pleasure is too much to bear. One more day of such a life is too long to live. Scripture tells us that we are granted "three score and ten years." Solomon asks, "Whether I am 30 or 70, is it worth going on? Would I have been better off as a stillborn?"

Where is the silver lining? We find the answer in chapter 6, verses 1 and 2. God grants us the means for pleasure on this earth. Yet he leaves it up to us to find the pleasure in his gifts. Solomon knew about God but didn't feel close to God. At times, it appears that he even resented the giver. If we resent the giver, if we distance ourselves from our maker, we may curse the gifts—even the gift of life. If we know and love

> Psychiatrists call the lack of feeling **anhedonia**. Give a woman with anhedonia a million dollars and she says, "That's nice"—yet barely lifts an eyebrow. Children and grandchildren come to visit and she says, "I appreciate them coming—but frankly I really don't care." Anhedonia is the cardinal symptom of severe depression.
>
> ☐

the giver, we find joy in the gifts, even during times of trouble.

☐ Reflection and Application

1. Most people question at times, even if the question is fleeting, whether it is worth going on with our lives. How does a Christian answer such questions?

2. In 6:11, Solomon suggests that we really cannot talk ourselves out of our misery and depression. How would you counter Solomon's argument?

A Closer Look

Ecclesiastes is, overall, a depressing book. Chapters 5 and 6 expose the depths of the wise king's dejection. How did he work himself into such a depressed mood? Solomon asked many questions, and the answer to each successive question depressed him even more than the previous one. He reflected upon the realities of existence and each reflection was progressively more painful. Some years ago, the existentialist philosopher Jean Paul Sartre wrote a novel entitled *Nausea*. The main character, like Solomon, looked deeper and deeper into himself and the world around. The more he looked, the more "sick with life" he became, sick to the point that he was literally nauseated with life. Both Solomon and Sartre's character felt despair to the point of a sickness near death because they could not see beyond the horizon of their own view. Contrast David, who, even in his despair, could still see above the horizon: "The Lord sits enthroned over the flood; the Lord is enthroned as King forever. The Lord gives strength to his people; the Lord blesses his people with peace" (Psalm 29:10, 11).

5
HOW CAN I FIND WISDOM?
Ecclesiastes 7:1-8:1

The Limits of Wise Sayings

Solomon shared more fragments of worldly wisdom in chapter 7. This passage reads like the book of Proverbs, yet the wise sayings are for the most part devoid of hope. For example, he introduced one section with "In this meaningless life..." (7:15). If life is meaningless, what is the value of a wise saying? Solomon didn't offer guidelines for the spiritual life such as Jesus offered in the Sermon on the Mount (Matthew 5-7). He exuded wisdom but didn't defend it. We must therefore take care when applying these proverbs to our lives. In fact, we should *always* take care when we apply any pithy, yet wise saying. My father used to remind me that "a rolling stone gathers no moss." Something to think about? Yes. A foundation upon which to build my relationship with God? No.

Ecclesiastes 7:1-9
A Sad Face is Good for the Heart

Solomon tells us to appreciate life, keep death in mind (7:1). Seek opportunities to "mourn with those who mourn" (7:2; Romans 12:15). Forget that happy face. A sad face is good for the heart (7:3). Given the choice, choose the company of a serious, truthful companion rather than one who only makes you laugh (7:5). Avoid excess. Play by the rules. Forcing money from someone or taking a bribe turns the wise toward foolishness and the pure towards corruption (7:7). Seek a patient, not a prideful heart (7:8). Hold your temper when someone provokes you (7:9). To sum up, seek a sober, balanced, and reflective life.

How interesting. Wise king Solomon encouraged us to "do as I say, not as I did." *He* didn't quench his desires; he indulged himself beyond our imaginations. He was among the most proud of men.

Solomon reminds me of the stoic Roman emperor Marcus Aurelius (AD 121-180). Compared to other Roman emperors and to Solomon, Marcus emanated wisdom, self-examination, restraint in thought, self-control in behavior, and purity of heart. No trace of Julius Caesar's ravenous ambition or Nero's brutally rampant hedonism can be found in Marcus. Yet Marcus was not a happy man. He believed the human soul stood naked and alone amidst the chaos and futility of the cosmos. Therefore, each person must constantly struggle to remain pure and undefiled.

Where did Marcus's stoicism guide him? Not to great leadership. He conquered few new lands. He brought no great reforms to the empire. He even selected Commodus as his successor, a ruler who became one of the most brutal and destructive in the history of the empire. The wisdom of Marcus comes to us in bits and pieces from his *Meditations*. He doesn't leave us a guidebook for life.

Both Solomon and Marcus divvy out pieces of the big picture of life. Neither gives us the big picture. Only by viewing life through the lens of God's love can we see the big picture. Even so, if we study these sayings, we discover some useful elements of the picture of life, a silver lining in this cloud. Here's one: Solomon advises that we do better when we accept criticism (7:5). I am a researcher. I submit articles to scientific journals so that my research can become available to others. For an article to be accepted for publication by a good scientific journal, other scientists must pass judgment on the article. Frequently my submissions are returned to me with cogent—and at times biting!—criticisms. However painful, I don't grow as a scientist if I don't open myself to criticism from people more wise than I.

> It is better to heed a wise man's rebuke than to listen to the song of fools.
>
> Ecclesiastes 7:5

☐ Reflection and Application

1. What does Solomon mean when he writes, "Sorrow is better than laughter, because a sad face is good for the heart"? Do you agree or not?

2. Give some reasons we experience difficulty in accepting criticism, even from persons whom we trust to be wise.

Ecclesiastes 7:10-14
Enjoy Each Good Day

In 7:10-14, Solomon returned to a theme he developed earlier in the book, that is, "seize the day." The psalmist wrote: "This is the day the Lord has made; let us rejoice and be glad in it" (Psalm 118:24). God continually reminds us that we mustn't dwell on the past nor trust too much in the future (that is, the future on this earth). God's time is the present and eternity. The wise person recognizes the value of each day; she doesn't look back, longing for the past, only to find herself numb to the beauty and joy of today (7:10). She tries not to fret about the future. If she worries about food on the table tomorrow, she can't enjoy the food on the table today.

Reveling in his wealth through much of his life, Solomon once again values wisdom over wealth at the end of his life (7:11-12). Money may appear to protect us, yet only God's wisdom sustains us. In Proverbs 3:18, we read that "[Wisdom] is a tree of life to those who embrace her." Money cannot bring such a blessing. Wisdom brings life by bringing us close to

God, to a more full understanding of his infinite ways. If we are wise, we seize the day, the day that the Lord has prepared for us (7:14).

☐ Reflection and Application

1. How often do you lose an hour, perhaps even a day, worrying about tomorrow or bemoaning yesterday? In what ways do you/can you overcome your worry?

2. Do you at times fret over money to the point that you can't enjoy a beautiful day or the company of good friends? How can you "seize the day" daily?

• *Ecclesiastes 7:15-22*
Life in the Balance

Solomon encouraged a life of balance. Don't be overly wicked. Don't be overly wise. Don't be overly righteous? How can we be overly *righteous?* We become overly righteous (7:16) when we become self-righteous, when we become proud in—and of—our righteousness. We lose our sense of balance when we forget that we're like the little girl in the nursery rhyme:

"There was a little girl who had a little curl that hung in the middle of her forehead. When she was good, she was very, very good, but when she was bad she was horrid." Jesus warned, "Be careful not to do your 'acts of righteousness' before men, to be seen by them. If you do, you will have no reward from your Father in heaven" (Matthew 6:1).

If we consider ourselves better than others, if we believe that others stand around in awe of us, praising us behind our backs, we are in for a rude awakening. Don't take praise too seriously that's said to our faces. We might just be shocked when we hear that those same persons have been criticizing us behind our backs (7:21). We do the same thing. We praise folks to their faces, and we criticize them when we think they can't hear us (7:22). The person who is wise realizes that others do to us as we do to them.

☐ Reflection and Application

1. All of us at times think more highly of ourselves than we ought. In what circumstances are you tempted to self-righteous thoughts?

2. What is a balanced Christian life? In what ways should Christians maintain balance, for example, in the use of their time?

Ecclesiastes 7:23-8:1
The Sources of Wisdom

Solomon searched for wisdom and found that wisdom couldn't be discovered (7:23, 24). Along the way, however, Solomon did learn a most important lesson, a silver lining among the clouds of an otherwise discouraging search. He learned that women mean trouble (7:28)! For Solomon, this was all too true. He loved many foreign women, and these women turned his heart to foreign gods (1 Kings 11:1-6). Perhaps he believed that women were the downfall of all men. If this was his conclusion, he, of course, was wrong. Women weren't the problem; they merely highlighted the source of his own personal weakness, his very large blind spot. He was blinded by the influence of *evil* women—and his kingdom divided during the next generation as a result.

If we wish to find wisdom, we must look for the blind spots in our lives. But let us hope that our search, unlike Solomon's, won't be too late. Discovering our blind spots late in life, after we have caused much damage and hurt to others, will be painful. Solomon was able to blunt his personal pain by rationalizing that all persons are corrupt (7:29). Misery, after all, loves company. I doubt, however, whether or not Solomon ever eliminated the pain of his sin and the discouragement of his ultimately failed enterprises. Few rulers began ruling with more reason to hope, and few rulers were more discouraged at the end of their reigns.

▯ Reflection and Application

1. In what ways did Solomon realize how much he had lost near the end of his life?

2. How can we discover our own blind spots?

A Closer Look

Throughout Ecclesiastes, Solomon reflected upon wisdom. Was wisdom of value or not? How do we find wisdom? What difference does it make? How will wisdom change our lives? As he discovered answers to these questions, the wise king became progressively more despondent. The wisdom of this world doesn't lead to happiness. Worldly wisdom is partial wisdom, and partial wisdom leads to discouragement. Only wisdom from God brings us the treasure of happiness.

Can't the search for wisdom lead to happiness? Solomon answered this question in Proverbs 2:3-6: "If you call out for insight and cry aloud for understanding... and search for it as for hidden treasure, then you will understand the fear of the Lord and find the knowledge of God. For the Lord gives wisdom and from his mouth come knowledge and understanding."

▯

6
HOW CAN I FIND JUSTICE?
Ecclesiastes 8:2-9:12

Obedience and Justice

Beginning in Chapter 8, Solomon encouraged obedience to the king, not because the king was good but because we take an oath before God to be obedient. We obey the king because we have made a covenant with God. Despite the amoral laws of nature and the unjust rule of kings, people who keep their covenant with God will, in the end, do better than people who don't. God's gift to those who keep their covenants is enjoyment of each day's work and marvel in the ways of God. Both good and bad rest in the hands of God. If we strain to understand the ways of God, if we strive to grasp the justice of God, we will be frustrated. The ways of God are above and beyond us. Simply thank God for what you possess and enjoy the good times granted you, for you don't know—can't know—how long those good times will last.

Ecclesiastes 8:1-9
Obey the Ruler, Regardless!

Christians dwelling in a democratic society constantly balance obedience to our laws and our leaders with protest, perhaps even civil disobedience. Paul admonished, "Everyone must submit himself to the governing authorities" (Romans 13:1, 2). We readily submit ourselves and criticize those who rebel when we agree with the policies of our leaders. When we don't agree, however, we become rebellious. For example, when a law is instituted that protects our children from pornography (a law with which we agree), we readily submit. On the other hand, if a law is passed that permits a sleazy nightclub to be built in our neighborhood, we march on the city council. Such protests are key to the workings of a democracy.

Solomon ruled during an era of almost absolute power for the king. Solomon therefore gave advice to servants of the king. *Even if* a servant thinks he is right and the king is wrong, remain quiet (8:3). After all, he might be wrong, and the king might be right (8:4). A better opportunity may come along later for registering his protest (8:5, 6). Things may change, and his protest will have been in vain (8:7). What difference will it make? He cannot control fate (8:8). Finally, he must not exert himself or try to lord anything over others, for he will only be hurt in the end (8:9).

If we follow Solomon's gloomy counsel literally, we might as well sit and take whatever happens to us. Yet there is a silver lining to this fatalistic cloud. Most of us become quite exercised about how our rulers are ruling. We spend hours and hours reading the newspapers, watching the news on TV, or listening to talk radio. The more we read and the more we listen, the more upset and angry we become. We stew within ourselves, and we argue with others. We forget Paul's admonition. Our leaders are established by *God*. God has used all sorts of leaders, from evil and aggressive despots in Assyria (Isaiah 8:1-10) to the benevolent rulers of Persia (Nehemiah 2:1-6). Those leaders he uses to work out his will at one time, he punishes at another (Isaiah 10:5-11). God is in charge, and we aren't wise enough to see the big picture. Solomon, as discouraged as he was, realized the will of God was beyond his comprehension.

☐ Reflection and Application

1. Solomon was king. How can we explain his admonition to obey the king? Was he speaking of his own subjects or of all rulers?

2. Do you find yourself fretting too often about politics? What steps might you, as a Christian, take to gain peace for yourself and justice in the world?

Ecclesiastes 8:10-17
The Meaning of History

Solomon encouraged the longer view. When we think about it, can we *see* good triumph over evil? Not really. Neither could Solomon. Though he trusted that things go better for the person who fears God (8:12), even he couldn't comprehend how good wins over evil (8:17). Even so, he dropped a pearl of wisdom during his musings: if you don't couple the punishment with the offense quickly, the punishment does little to deter bad behavior (8:11). Most of us learned this lesson when we raised our children. If we don't punish them immediately after they grab a cookie, they don't learn to keep their hands off when we say "No cookies until after dinner." Overall, however, Solomon didn't believe that we could make sense of current or past events: "No one can comprehend what goes on under the sun" (8:17). We cannot find meaning. It makes no difference whether we are wise or not. We simply cannot comprehend, according to the wise king. Is there a silver lining in this cloud?

Yes, we should take hope that we can't always comprehend the happenings around us. If we could

> Though the mills of God grind slowly, yet they
> grind exceedingly small;
> Though with patience he stands waiting, with
> exactness grinds he all.
> -"The Mills of God," Henry W. Longfellow
> []

comprehend all events, if we were able to see current and historical happenings through the eyes of God, then we would *be* God. Let me tell you: if I were God, the world would truly be in one fine mess!

Years ago, my wife and I served as medical missionaries in Cameroon. We faced a major struggle with the local and national government. In fact, we were asked to shut down our medical mission efforts. I wrote a letter to the mission committee of our supporting church, complaining of our fate. How could we be stopped from providing medical care and spiritual food to these hurting and starving people? The chair of the committee wrote back, quoting "The Mills of God" by Longfellow. He reminded me that God's timing isn't ours, and his results are often beyond our expectations. He was correct: a few weeks later, we gained permission to continue our work—with legal protection that has sustained the work in Cameroon to this day. During those weeks of waiting, I thought "the mills of God" had stopped producing for us. I was wrong; God's mills were grinding at his pace, not mine. He solved a problem for 30 years that I impatiently wanted fixed within 30 days.

□ Reflection and Application

1. Do you at times think about what a mess the world is in today? If so, during what other periods of

history (including biblical history) did the world seem in a greater mess than it is today? How did those terrible times turn out?

2. Can you recall periods of history in the Bible during which God's timetable was very slow, yet more perfect than we could have imagined? Consider, for example, the centuries between the Old Testament prophets and the birth of Christ.

Ecclesiastes 9:1-12
All Share a Common Destiny

Could wise Solomon's dejection dip any deeper? Yes. In Chapter 9, he concluded that the living know that they are going to die and they cannot get away from that knowledge (9:5). That's the good news! To make matters worse, up until the time we die, we hold no idea and no control over what will happen to us: "All share a common destiny" (9:2). Is it better to be alive or dead? Solomon proposed that the living are better off than the dead, for "Anyone who is among the living has hope" (9:4). Even the memory of those who once lived and live no more is forgotten (9:5). All of the passions of the dead, both good and bad, vanish (9:6). Herein we find the silver lining.

Better that we enjoy each day we are granted to live (a theme to which Solomon returned time and again). After all, it's better to be a live dog than a dead lion (9:4)! For this reason, enjoy your meals (9:7), take care of yourself (9:8), enjoy your loved ones (9:9), and enjoy your work (9:10). God has given you today without promising you tomorrow. Take your time (9:11); stop and smell the flowers; "The race is not to the swift." You may not be here tomorrow, for evil may trap you at any time (9:12). God has given you today. Enjoy!

Solomon discovered truth—but not the whole truth. Compare his view of joy and hope with his father David's: "Surely goodness and mercy will follow me all the days of my life, and I will dwell in the house of the Lord forever" (Psalm 23:6). God is more than "just there." He is our father. He sent us a savior. He guides us. He cares for us. He is the God who will be with us now and forever.

▢ Reflection and Application

1. Solomon could see no difference in the way God treated good or evil people on this earth. Do you believe that evil people on earth fare about the same as good people? If so, give an example.

2. List some reasons Solomon couldn't see God's love and mercy.

A Closer Look

Chapters 8 and 9 of Ecclesiastes are among the most depressing in Scripture. How on earth did these thoughts ever become part of our sacred text? I believe that Solomon lost hope, and God wished us to recognize the consequences of such a loss. Solomon failed to trust God. Loss of hope takes us down about as far as we can go. God gave us Ecclesiastes so that we would wait, with both patience and hope, for God to work his will on earth and in heaven.

> God gave us Ecclesiastes in part to warn us of the poverty in our lives—in the midst of wealth—when we place our hope in wealth rather than God.
>
> ❏

7
HOW WILL I RECOGNIZE WISDOM WHEN I SEE IT?

Ecclesiastes 9:13-10:20

Seeing Wisdom is Believing

Solomon saw much foolishness around him. He also recognized wisdom when he saw it. The wise recognize examples of wisdom in others. After all, foolishness doesn't reign everywhere. How can we recognize wise actions scattered among the foolish ways of humankind? Stop. Look. Listen. Stop in a small city. Look for an insignificant person. Listen to that person's story. Don't focus on the rich and the powerful. Pay attention to the actions of a woman, not her words. Listen to a man who speaks softly and kindly, yet sparsely. Wisdom leads to good works, and good works bear fruit. Foolish acts lead nowhere.

Some years ago, a local minister referred an older woman to me for treatment. He said she was depressed and obsessed with things beyond her control. She was depressed, yet not in the way I expected. Rather, she was very concerned about the tribal warfare in Rwanda. The church had ignored her request to support a war relief effort in that country where hundreds of thousands were killed or mutilated. At night she prayed for these people and during the day she wrote letters and called acquaintances to collect money for the relief effort. Over time, she collected a few thousand dollars that she forwarded to missionaries in the area. After I heard her story, I encouraged her to continue the relief efforts but to recognize that most people would turn a deaf ear. This "insignificant" woman was one of the most wise and most caring I have ever known (9:15).

Ecclesiastes 9:13-18
Wisdom is Better than Strength

Where can we find examples of wisdom? How will we recognize wise acts when we see them? Perhaps a man with little power saves a city, a man that we don't remember later. Solomon may refer in this passage to an event during the reign of his father, David (2 Samuel 20:15-22). A troublemaker, Sheba, rebelled against David. This troublemaker soon realized that he couldn't overpower the commander of David's army, Joab. Sheba fled to the city of Abel Beth Maacah. Joab pursued him and surrounded the city, set up a siege ramp, and began to beat down the gate. A wise woman asked to speak with Joab. She reasoned with him: "You are trying to destroy a city that is a mother in Israel" (2 Samuel 20:19). Joab replied that he didn't wish to destroy the city but only to destroy Sheba, the enemy of David. The woman promised to throw the head of Sheba over the wall if only Joab would spare the city.

Joab agreed and Sheba's head was cut off and delivered to Joab; Abel Beth Macaah was saved.

We remember the warrior king David. We remember the skilled general Joab. We don't remember the wise woman who saved a small city. She saved it by quiet and reasoned words, pleading with Joab not to extend his vengeance toward Sheba onto an entire city. To put it in Old Testament terms, "if there is serious injury, you are to take life for life, eye for an eye..." (Exodus 21:15). Joab must not take one hundred eyes for one.

As Christians, we are encouraged to forgive those who harm us, to turn the other cheek (Matthew 5:38-41). Yet we retain a desire for justice in our society. In our zeal for justice, for assuring that our cities are safe and our rights are protected, don't we at times want to make examples of the guilty? Do the punishments we demand always fit the crime? Solomon reminds us that, in secular judgment, the punishment should fit the crime.

☐ Reflection and Application

1. Can you think of situations in history when powerful rulers have been personally injured or affronted and then have extended their vengeance far beyond the "an eye for an eye" type of revenge?

2. Do you have some thoughts as to why people such as the wise woman in 2 Samuel are forgotten and so many foolish rulers are remembered for millennia?

Ecclesiastes 10:1-11
Strive to Live Rationally in an Irrational World

Solomon saw foolishness and irrational behavior everywhere he looked. Unlike Jesus, who encourages us to be a bright light unto the world (Matthew 5: 14), Solomon believed a little folly at times has more influence than all the light of wisdom could spread (10: 1). For this reason, we who desire to be wise must take care how we live in the midst of folly. For example, those in positions of authority can harm us if they become angry with us (10:4). We must remain calm and keep doing our jobs even when the authorities order us to do things we find idiotic (10:6).

Solomon encouraged us to take caution, because an irrational world can be a dangerous world. Take care if we dig a pit; we may fall into it (10:8)! If we don't take care, we may be injured and then we will be of no value to anyone, much less to ourselves (10:11).

Solomon reminded his readers that this world is not our home. Unfortunately, he didn't offer much hope for a better world. The writer of the book of

Hebrews (in Chapter 11) recounted the wanderings of Abraham. The world was not a rational place for the father of Israel. He was forced to leave his home in Ur. He lived in tents rather than in a permanent home. Even so, Abraham "was looking forward to the city with foundations, whose architect and builder is God" (Hebrews 11:10).

Unlike Solomon, who never escaped the world's absurdity, Abraham recognized something beyond the irrationality of happenings around him. He recognized that God could intervene in this world in miraculous ways. Abraham became a father to Isaac long after he and Sarah had passed through the childbearing years. Through Isaac, the nation of Israel grew to numbers "as countless as the sand on the seashore" (Hebrews 11:12).

☐ Reflection and Application

1. Most of us have had the experience of looking around and commenting, "I can't believe how crazy people act." Discuss some ways in which the world today just seems like a crazy place.

2. Why do you think Solomon had so much difficulty seeing beyond the irrationality of this world?

Ecclesiastes 10:12-14
The Words of the Wise are Gracious

Most of us find Ecclesiastes difficult to read. The book is filled with paradoxes. In places, he wrote that we must value wisdom (9:18); in other places, he wrote that with much wisdom comes much sorrow (1:18). What are we to conclude from such foggy logic (if it can be called logic at all)? We find the silver lining in this fog by comparing the paradox of Solomon's advice with his practice. Solomon was guilty of the very thing he warned his readers against. He couldn't stop writing, as if he was consumed by his own words (10:12). He wrote so many "wise sayings" that the wise sayings contradict themselves. He multiplied word upon word about the gloomy future (10:14). Solomon predicted many evils to come (1:3-5; 1:9; 3:19). Yet he also wrote, "No one knows what is coming…" (10:14).

☐ Reflection and Application

1. Ever heard the expression, "he talked himself into a corner"? Can you remember such a time in your own life?

2. What is "gracious" speech (10:12)?

Ecclesiastes 10:15-20
The Life of the Wise Under a Foolish Ruler

Thousands of years have passed since the days of Solomon. Some things, however, never change. Corrupt leadership curses many nations. Solomon warned that corrupt leaders act like children (the Hebrew word *naar* in 10:16 is probably best translated child rather than servant). Solomon, though he probably didn't know it at the time, accurately describes his own son, Rehoboam. Solomon's grandson, Abijah, called Rehoboam *naar* (2 Chronicles 13:7). Rehoboam was one of the most corrupt and childish leaders in Judah's history (Read 1 Kings 12:1-15). A childish ruler attends to his pleasures rather than disciplining himself for leadership (10:16, 17). A childish ruler is lazy. While he enjoys himself, the nation decays (10:18). He lavishes money on his own pleasure rather than facing the problems of the nation head on (10:19). Worst of all, a childish king is dangerous. He is suspicious of everyone and places his spies everywhere. Even your own bedroom is not safe (10:20).

Solomon couldn't even trust his own behavior and perhaps for that reason he warned the readers of Ecclesiastes not to trust in worldly leaders. We wish to look up to our leaders, even to view them as father figures. We want to trust them. We may feel a little less secure, yet we will actually be more secure, if take

Solomon's advice. We should place our confidence where that confidence is best placed (John 14:1), namely with our Father in heaven through our Lord Jesus Christ!

☐ Reflection and Application

1. Have you placed your trust in human leadership, only to be disappointed? What led you to put your trust in the wrong place?

2. List some ways in which wise king Solomon acted as a child. Ever been there yourself?

A Closer Look

The various proverbs and maxims found in this section of Ecclesiastes might best be considered a loosely collected group of notes jotted down at odd times by an elderly king who is trying to make some sense of his life and to warn others of the pitfalls he encountered. We find silver linings among these mostly pessimistic warnings, yet we can never be certain that Solomon himself was comforted. Somehow the most wise of Old Testament characters never seems to have seen the big picture. He knew a lot *about* God. He didn't *know* God.

8
HOW CAN I BE SUCCESSFUL?
Ecclesiastes 11:1-10

Take Advantage of Your Youth

God promises us about seventy years of life. We, in the United States, have extended life expectancy to around 80 (that is, over one-half of us alive today will live at least until we are 80). Women live even a little longer than men. Scientists are working diligently to extend the life span even further. We have made slow but steady progress toward lengthening our lives and improving the quality of our lives.

Do we want to live forever? No. We want to remain young as long as possible. Immortality without the fountain of youth is not a pleasant prospect. Solomon encouraged us to take advantage of our youth. First, we should take advantage of the opportunities of youth, opportunities that may never come to us again (11:1, 8).

We should also try to find happiness during our youth. Solomon didn't encourage us to party until we drop—though I suspect he partied plenty. Rather, he encouraged the young to cherish their freedom from anxiety and care (11:10), to work diligently (11:6), and to enjoy the beauty of the day God gives. If you're young, don't look too far to the future (11:9). In Chapter 3 he wrote, "I know that there is nothing better for men than to be happy and do good while they live. That every man may eat and drink and find satisfaction in all his toil—this is the gift of God" (3:12, 13).

Ecclesiastes 11:1-5
Cast your Bread upon the Waters

God gives each of us windows of opportunity, not just for our own benefit but also for the benefit of others. In other words, God gives us opportunities to help others. We should take those opportunities when they come; after all, such opportunities won't always present themselves to us. When we bake more bread than we require personally, we must cast that bread on the waters (11:1). If we delay, waiting for perhaps an even greater opportunity, then the present opportunities may be lost. Many who read this section of Ecclesiastes assume that Solomon was writing about good business practices. His advice may apply to business, but Solomon was speaking about charitable works. Solomon conveyed some bad news and some good news. Here's the bad news: we can never predict what will happen in the future, and we can never understand the ways of God. He may bless us for a few years, after which we may lose everything (11:5). We have limited opportunities to help others. Therefore we should be quick to give and not wait until our coffers are full to execute our benevolence. Our benevolence fund is not bottomless.

Does Solomon's advice make sense for our church benevolence programs? We must be good stewards of the money and goods we give to others. But how can we know that the money we give or the food we provide *really* helps the people whom we wish to help? Shouldn't we be more careful about what we give and to whom we give it?

The good news is that Solomon provides us a partial answer, a silver lining to this frustrating picture of benevolence: "Cast your bread on the waters" (11:1). Don't worry if the bread floats out of sight and you see no benefit derive from your generosity. You may never know the influence of this or any of your gifts. The receiver may show no gratitude for years; however, at some time in the future you may learn that not only was the gift remembered, but it changed the person's life. A man I know stole a $200 television and was, months later, pricked by his guilt and began to turn his life around in another city. Years later, I met him on the street and he couldn't wait to tell me how he turned his life around, how he was so ashamed but now had the courage to face me. He gave me $200 on the spot to help someone else.

☐ Reflection and Application

1. How would you describe your attitude toward benevolence? Do you "cast your bread on the waters" or do you "watch the wind"?

2. Consider how we can be good stewards of God's gifts to us and at the same time give money, food, and clothing away to people who may waste those gifts.

Ecclesiastes 11:6
Sow your Seed in the Morning

My father was an early riser. While the rest of my family slept, he awakened and left the house by five o'clock; after all, "The early bird gets the worm." Solomon, however, was not writing about early birds in Ecclesiastes 11:6; he was writing about being prepared for the breaks we get in life. Opportunities come in the morning when we arrive at work and they come in the late afternoon when we're preparing to leave our work. They come to the young, and they come to the old (11:6).

One of my favorite biblical characters is Caleb. When Caleb was very old, he had earned the right to relax. After all, he had delivered the minority report detailing Canaan's bounty that encouraged Joshua to lead Israel in the conquest of the promised land (Numbers 13:26-30). Rather than relaxing in his old age, however, he approached Joshua with the following proposition: "I am still as strong today as the day Moses sent me out... Now give me this hill country that the Lord promised me that day" (Joshua 14:11, 12). There was just one problem. The hill country, Hebron, was still possessed by the Canaanites. At the age of eighty-five, he saw an opportunity, and he seized that opportunity to conquer Hebron for Israel. Caleb didn't rest during the evening of his life. We, like Caleb, should give a full *life's* work.

☐ Reflection and Application

1. What are your retirement plans? Might Caleb influence you in some way?

2. Most of us experience "down" times at our work, times when we simply are not productive. How have you missed opportunities in this way?

Ecclesiastes 11:7-10

Remember Your Creator While You are Young

Solomon warns that evil days lie ahead (12:1). Youth is the time of life to enjoy God's gift of life. Once again, he encouraged the reader to "seize the day," for no one can be assured of tomorrow. When the sun rises in the morning (11:7), that is the time to enjoy the beauty of God's creation, to set one's anxieties aside. We don't know when the days of darkness will return. When they do, we may not see light again for a very long time (11:8). Enjoy the morning of your life. Take care, however. If you use the good day God grants you for evil activities, God will surely bring judgment on you (11:9). Don't fret about what will happen to you in the future. Take care of your body if you want to ward off the days of darkness (11:10a).

Have you ever worried about something to the point that you couldn't sleep? Perhaps you've worried about a relationship that turned sour or worried about losing your job. Among the most miserable feelings I've ever felt is lying wide awake in bed, hour after hour, worrying so much that I can't sleep, looking at the clock a hundred times.

Then morning gradually breaks through. The sky lightens, birds begin to sing, and I feel better. Morning is a time of hope, a time we can feel closer to God:

"Morning by morning, O Lord, you hear my voice; morning by morning, I lay my requests before you and wait in expectation" (Psalm 5:3). Solomon knew the beauty and hope of the morning. He regretted that he had wasted the morning of his life. For him, youth and vigor had been meaningless.

☐ Reflection and Application

1. How might your thoughts run away from you during a sleepless night? How did you feel when you first saw the light of day?

2. Do you agree with Solomon that youth is the best time of life? If so, give some reasons. If not, how would you refute Solomon?

A Closer Look

Solomon is a fatalist. Was Solomon justified in his negative attitude? While some of Solomon's projects came to naught during his life, others bore much fruit. Looking back, he couldn't have predicted which of his actions would prove successful and which would not. He couldn't have predicted, for instance, that thousands of years later the Jews would return to Jerusalem and venerate the foundation of "Solomon's temple" (the

Wailing Wall) as the most sacred site in the world. We must not be overly cautious; we must be willing to take chances, if not for ourselves, then certainly for others. We never know which of our projects will be successful or even if they'll be successful at all. As the old saying goes, "Nothing ventured, nothing gained."

9
ARE THE GOLDEN YEARS REALLY GOLDEN?

Ecclesiastes 12:1-14

Old Age – The Days of Trouble

Worldly wisdom grows decrepit with age. Old age, in turn, taints worldly wisdom. Solomon wrote Ecclesiastes when he was near death, when he experienced the infirmities of late life. He had ruled Israel for 40 years when he died (I Kings 11:42); most people during Solomon's rule didn't live nearly so long.

Even so, Solomon discovered a silver lining in the "clouds [that] return after the rain" (12:2). Through all

Today, most of us will live as long or longer than Solomon. Nearly 12% of the people in the USA are 65 and older. The median age of persons in the USA is over 80 years (that is, over one-half of us will live beyond the age of 80). If a woman lives to the age of 65, on average she will live another 20 years (men will, on average, live another 16 years after 65). Most of these late years are "golden years." Older persons in the USA are healthy, happy, active, and better off economically than at any time in our history. Even so, we face many challenges, such as the maintenance of Social Security and Medicare (American elders depend heavily on both). And as we grow old, we do become more decrepit.

the miseries of life, especially the miseries of late life, we must remember our Creator. There are seeds of truth in Solomon's glum description of late life. When things go well, some of us ignore God. In times of suffering, however, we turn to God. God whispers to us perhaps in youth—but he sometimes shouts to us in later life; *then* we remember our Creator. If we are wise in the ways of God, however, we will remember him in our youth as well.

Ecclesiastes 12:1-5
When the Keepers of the House Tremble

Solomon's poetic symbolism peaks in Chapter 12 as he provides one of the most graphic, humorous, yet depressing descriptions of late life to be found in the world's literature. The last days of our lives are "days of trouble" (12:1). These are days of few pleasures. Late life is the winter of life, the final desolate landscape, the time when evening comes quickly and "the sun and the light and the moon and the stars grow dark" (12:2). Trouble follows trouble as we age, for "clouds return after the rain." Elderly persons lose their balance, are unsteady on their feet, and their hands tremble when they attempt to write something on a piece of paper: "The keepers of the house tremble" (12:3a).

Arthritis takes its toll and "strong men stoop" (12:3b). Our teeth, which in our youth tore through a good steak, fall out of our mouths; so now we're reduced to eating cream of wheat for "the grinders cease because they are few" (12:3c). In times past, we could gaze through a window and almost count every leaf on every tree. In later life, even the *trees* are blurred: "Those looking through the windows grow dim" (12:3d). Cataracts are common among the elderly, distorting and blocking vision.

Did You Know?

Because there were no false teeth during the time of Solomon, decayed teeth often led to poor nutrition, hastening the death of older people.

We eat and eat, yet our bowels don't move. Constipation leads to hemorrhoids, laxatives, and bloating, for "the doors to the street are closed" (12:4a)! Older people sleep fitfully, wake frequently, and wake finally at an earlier hour than they used to (12:4b). What do you do when you wake up early, especially if you don't have anything much to do? Some stay in their beds, depressed over the prospects of their lives. Even the songs of the birds that greet the sunrise do not cheer (12:4c): "Men rise up at the sound of the birds but all their songs grow faint."

Late life can be a fearful time; as older people lose their balance, walking down stairs is an anxious prospect: "Men are afraid of heights" (12:5a). Older people are also less able to protect themselves. If they live in a city, the necessity of going to the store to shop becomes a fearful task: "Men are afraid of...the dangers in the streets" (12:5b).

There is perhaps no better marker of late life than gray or white hair: "The almond tree blossoms" (12:5c). The almond tree, unlike most other trees, blossoms in winter on a leafless stem. Its flowers, initially a pale pink color, turn white as they fall from its branches. Even if the older person looks fit enough physically, she acts her age. We expect a grasshopper to jump and spring into action as we near it. What a surprise when the grasshopper "drags himself along" (12:5d). Finally, things that should matter to the older person just *don't*. The most telling symptom of depression among the elderly is a lack of interest. The depressed older man will say, "I know I should enjoy the grandkids when they visit, but frankly I just don't care." Or to put it another way, "desire is no longer stirred" (12:5e).

> Then man goes to his eternal home and mourners go about the streets.
> Ecclesiastes 12:5f

To what does the older person look forward? To death, to a return to his origins (12:5f). Solomon waffles as he concludes Ecclesiastes. When he speaks of an eternal home, it is far from certain that he refers to an everlasting life with God. As we see below, Solomon, in some ways, views life as a cycle—we are born, we live, and we die—and that's the end of the matter.

As we complete our reading of Ecclesiastes 12:1-5, we're left with about as depressing a view of late life as Solomon could picture. Late life at the threshold of the

21st century in the United States may not validate his picture, however. Most of us will remain healthy and active until perhaps even the last months of our lives. Though the ravages of memory loss from diseases such as Alzheimer's are a frightening prospect, new therapies appear to be just around the corner, aids that will reduce the burden of dementia. We are learning more each day about ways to assist the functionally impaired elderly to live as independently as possible. Late life may not be as depressing as Solomon describes.

☐ Reflection and Application

1. After reading Ecclesiastes 12:1-5, do you have any different interpretations of Solomon's figurative language regarding late life from that which I've presented? Use your imagination; symbolic language is meant to stimulate your imagination!

2. Discuss your expectations for your later years regarding health and quality of life.

Ecclesiastes 12:6-8
At the Threshold of Death

In 12:6, Solomon continues his sad tale of aging to its climax—death. Light is life. The silver cord holds the lamp that provides the light in a tent or room. Once broken, the lamp falls and the light goes out. The cord is the thread of life and the thread is severed (12:6a). The water of life is contained in the body. Once the body is broken, shattered like a pitcher at the well, life ceases (12:6b). Water is drawn from a well by an apparatus consisting of a wheel and rope attached to a container. Once the wheel is broken, water can no longer be drawn (12:6c); without water, life ceases.

At death, the body returns to the elements from which it was created, "from dust to dust" (12:7a). The identity of the body dissolves into the earth. Before we developed methods to embalm the body after death (the Egyptians embalmed their dead, but the Israelites did not), death certainly led quickly to the body's disintegration. The spirit returns to God (12:8). Solomon appears more certain of our fate in this passage than he did in 3:21. For Solomon, the spirit returning to God is not a joyous occasion but rather the final quenching of life. No wonder he cries once again, "Meaningless, meaningless!" (12:8); for this wise king, there is no silver lining to the looming death cloud, only a silver cord which is broken. God breathed his Spirit and there was life: "When you send your Spirit, they are created" (Psalm 104:30); when the Spirit is taken away, life ceases: "When you hide your face, they are terrified; when you take away their breath, they die and return to the dust" (Psalm 104:29).

What a difference life in Christ makes! Paul wrote, "Where, O death, is your victory? Where, O death, is your sting?" The sting of death is sin and the power of death is the law. But thanks be to God! He gives us the victory through our Lord Jesus Christ... your labor in the Lord is not in vain" (1 Corinthians 15:55-58).

☐ Reflection and Application

1. If death meant dissolution or entry into some nether world to you, would you react in the same way as Solomon?

2. Does life sometimes seem to you as fragile as a silver cord that can easily break, or a pitcher at a well that can easily be shattered? How fragile do you feel life is? Describe what gives life its permanence and stability.

Ecclesiastes 12:9-14
The Conclusion of the Matter

The wise king pondered almost every aspect of life (12:9,10). In the end, however, he felt the need to draw some conclusion. He wished to leave a clear message. He wished his words to be like nails hammered into the wall, something on which to hang the experiences of life, fixed points in an otherwise fluid world (12:11). He realized, however, that his words could be lost among the many sayings and books of both the wise and the foolish. He also realized that much reading doesn't necessarily mean *good* reading: "Of making many books, there is no end, and much study wearies the body." Therefore Solomon left us a take-home message, "Fear God and keep his commandments, for this is the whole duty of man" (12:13). No one escapes the judgment of God (12:14). That is the conclusion of the matter for Solomon.

We must keep our eyes focused upon God, and we must never lose sight of God's will for us, our duty toward him, and his final judgment. Solomon's silver lining proclaims a truth, but not the whole truth. He fails to notice a vision of God, a truth that didn't escape his father David: "I trust in your unfailing love; my heart rejoices in your salvation. I will sing to the Lord, for he has been good to me" (Psalm 13:5, 6). Worldly wisdom knows God's power and judgment, but it doesn't know God's love. The warrior king David, the frequently fallible David, knew love.

☐ Reflection and Application

1. Describe Solomon's view of humankind's relationship with God. Does Solomon find hope in God?

2. Do you believe that we can study too much? Have you so thoroughly studied a confusing topic that you became even more confused? Read 1 Corinthians 13:8.

A Closer Look

Ecclesiastes is a difficult book to study. Just as Solomon warns that "of making many books there is no end," there have been many books written to help us understand Ecclesiastes. To gain better insight into this confusing book, however, we must read between the lines, we must search for the silver lining. One of the most helpful means for finding that silver lining is to compare Ecclesiastes to the psalms of David. Solomon's father grasped a vision of God that seems to have forever escaped the king granted by God the greatest worldly wisdom of all time.

About the Author
Dan Blazer

Dan Blazer, MD, MPH, Ph.D., is JP Gibbons Professor of Psychiatry at Duke University School of Medicine and former Dean of Medical Education in Durham, North Carolina. He and his wife Sherrill are members of the Brooks Avenue Church of Christ in Raleigh, North Carolina. This devotional guide was written while Dan was on sabbatical as a Fellow at the Center for Advanced Studies in the Behavioral Sciences, Stanford University, Palo Alto, California.